Survival and Migration Route Probabilities of Juvenile Chinook Salmon in the Sacramento-San Joaquin River Delta during the Winter of 2009–10

By Russell W. Perry, Jason G. Romine, and Scott J. Brewer, U.S. Geological Survey; Peter E. LaCivita, William N. Brostoff, U.S. Army Corps of Engineers; and Eric D. Chapman, University of California at Davis

Prepared in cooperation with the
U.S. Fish and Wildlife Service

Open-File Report 2012-1200

U.S. Department of the Interior
U.S. Geological Survey

U.S. Department of the Interior
KEN SALAZAR, Secretary

U.S. Geological Survey
Marcia K. McNutt, Director

U.S. Geological Survey, Reston, Virginia: 2012

For product and ordering information:
World Wide Web: http://www.usgs.gov/pubprod
Telephone: 1-888-ASK-USGS

For an overview of USGS information products, including maps, imagery, and publications,
visit http://www.usgs.gov/pubprod

To order this and other USGS information products, visit http://store.usgs.gov

Suggested citation:
Perry, R.W., Romine, J.G., Brewer, S.J., LaCivita, P.E., Brostoff, W.N., and Chapman, E.D., 2012,
Survival and migration route probabilities of juvenile Chinook salmon in the Sacramento-San Joaquin
River Delta during the winter of 2009–10: U.S. Geological Survey Open-File Report 2012-1200, 30 p.

Contents

Figures

Tables

Conversion Factors

Multiply	By	To obtain
Length		
foot (ft)	0.3048	meter (m)
mile (mi)	1.609	kilometer (km)
Area		
square foot (ft^2)	0.09290	square meter (m^2)
Volume		
cubic foot (ft^3)	0.02832	cubic meter (m^3)
Flow rate		
cubic foot per second (ft^3/s)	0.02832	cubic meter per second (m^3/s)

Temperature in degrees Celsius (°C) may be converted to degrees Fahrenheit (°F) as follows:°F=(1.8×°C)+32.
Temperature in degrees Fahrenheit (°F) may be converted to degrees Celsius (°C) as follows:°C=(°F-32)/1.8

Survival and Migration Route Probabilities of Juvenile Chinook Salmon in the Sacramento-San Joaquin River Delta during the Winter of 2009–10

By Russell W. Perry, Jason G. Romine, and Scott J. Brewer, U.S. Geological Survey; Peter E. LaCivita, William N. Brostoff, U.S. Army Corps of Engineers; and Eric D. Chapman, University of California at Davis

Abstract

Juvenile Chinook salmon (*Oncorhynchus tshawytscha*) emigrating from natal tributaries of the Sacramento River may use a number of migration routes to negotiate the Sacramento-San Joaquin River Delta (hereafter, "the Delta"), each of which may influence their probability of surviving. We applied a mark-recapture model to data from acoustically tagged juvenile late-fall Chinook salmon that migrated through the Delta during the winter of 2009–10 (hereafter, 2010). This report presents findings from our fourth year of research.

We estimated route-specific survival for four release groups: two release groups that migrated through the Delta in December 2009 and January 2010, and two release groups that migrated during February 2010. Population-level survival through the Delta (S_{Delta}) ranged from 0.374 (SE = 0.040) to 0.524 (SE = 0.034) among releases. Although river flows for the February release groups were substantially higher (20,000–40,000 ft^3/s at Freeport) than for the December release groups (about 10,000 ft^3/s), S_{Delta} did not differ considerably between release groups. Among migration routes, fish migrating through the Sacramento River exhibited the highest survival, and fish entering the interior Delta exhibited the lowest survival. Fish entering Sutter and Steamboat Sloughs had lower survival than fish entering the Sacramento River during December, but similar survival during February. These patterns were consistent among release groups, and strikingly similar to patterns observed in previous years.

Migration routing varied among release groups partly because of differences in river discharge between releases. For the two December release groups, 26.5 and 28.9 percent of fish entered the interior Delta; for the two February release groups, 10.4 and 17.9 percent of fish entered the interior Delta. Differences in routing probabilities between December and February are partly related to the inverse relationship between flow and the fraction of discharge entering the interior Delta. The proportion of fish diverted into the interior Delta also can be affected by the status of the Delta Cross Channel's gates. The fraction of fish entering Sutter and Steamboat Sloughs also varied considerably among release groups from 22.1 to 44.7 percent, and did not appear correlated to river discharge. For example, the lowest and highest proportion of fish entering Sutter and Steamboat Sloughs occurred during February. Because fish entering Sutter and Steamboat Sloughs bypass the entrance to the interior Delta, a high proportion of fish migrating into this route reduces the proportion of fish entering the interior Delta.

Introduction

Many stocks of Chinook salmon (*Oncorhynchus tshawytscha*) in California, Washington, and Oregon are listed as threatened or endangered under the Endangered Species Act (Nehlsen and others, 1991; Myers and others, 1998). In the Central Valley of California, the winter, spring, and fall/late fall runs of Chinook salmon are federally listed as endangered, threatened, and "species of concern," respectively (National Marine Fisheries Service, 1997). Recently, due to below-target returns of fall Chinook salmon to the Sacramento River, the National Marine Fisheries Service declared a Federal Disaster and closed the 2008 salmon fishery along the West Coast (National Oceanic and Atmospheric Administration, 2008). Understanding factors affecting survival of salmon is critical to developing effective recovery strategies for these populations.

An important stage in the life history of Chinook salmon is the period of migration from natal tributaries to the ocean, when mortality of juvenile salmon in the Sacramento River may increase from a host of anthropogenic and natural factors (Baker and Morhardt, 2001; Brandes and McLain, 2001; Williams, 2006). Juvenile Chinook salmon emigrating from the Sacramento River must pass through the Sacramento-San Joaquin River Delta (hereafter, "the Delta"), a complex network of natural and man-made river channels linking the Sacramento River with San Francisco Bay (Nichols and others, 1986). Juvenile salmon may migrate through a number of routes on their journey to the ocean—for example, they may migrate within the mainstem Sacramento River leading directly into San Francisco Bay (see Route A in fig. 1). However, juvenile salmon also may migrate through longer secondary routes such as the interior Delta, the network of channels to the south of the mainstem Sacramento River (see Routes C and D in fig. 1). Juvenile salmon entering the interior Delta also are exposed to entrainment at water pumping projects in the southern Delta, which may decrease survival of fish using this migratory pathway (Kjelson and others, 1981; Brandes and McLain, 2001; Newman and Rice, 2002; Newman, 2003; Kimmerer, 2008; Newman, 2008; Newman and Brandes, 2010).

There is limited understanding of how water management actions in the Delta affect the population distribution and the route-specific survival of juvenile salmon. To address these uncertainties, we developed a mark-recapture model to estimate the route-specific components of population-level survival for acoustically tagged, late-fall Chinook smolts migrating through the Delta (Perry and others, 2010). This study provided the first quantitative estimates of route-specific survival through the Delta, and of the fraction of the population that uses each migration route. Furthermore, we explicitly quantified the relative contribution of each migration route to population-level survival. As with other authors (Newman and Brandes, 2010), we found that survival of fish migrating through the interior Delta was lower than survival of fish migrating through the Sacramento River. The proportion of the population entering the interior Delta differed between releases, which can influence population-level survival by shifting a fraction of the population from a low-survival migration route (the interior Delta) to a high-survival route (the Sacramento River). However, differences between releases in population-level survival were caused by changes in survival for given migration routes. These findings indicated that variation in population-level survival was driven both by variation in movement among routes and survival within routes.

In this report, we estimate survival and migration route probabilities for acoustically tagged late-fall Chinook salmon migrating through the Delta during the winter of 2009–10 (hereafter, 2010). This report presents survival estimates of the study's fourth consecutive year, providing important insights into interannual variations in route-specific survival and movement through the Delta. Design aspects of our previous study were maintained, but some aspects differed from previous years. The primary difference in study design between 2010 and previous years is the number of release groups, release timing, and release locations. Two releases were conducted in migration years 2007–09—one in December when the Delta Cross Channel was open, and one in January when the Delta Cross Channel was closed. An additional group of fish also was released into Georgiana Slough in 2008 and 2009 to increase sample sizes of fish migrating through the interior Delta. In comparison, for the 2010 migration year, two releases were conducted in December 2009, each consisting of two release locations (40 km upstream of Freeport at the Elkhorn boat ramp in the Sacramento River and in Georgiana Slough). The release at the Elkhorn Boat Ramp was farther upstream than the releases made near Sacramento in previous years. The release in early December was conducted when the Delta Cross Channel was open, and the later release in December was conducted when the Delta Cross Channel was closed. In addition, tagged fish released in December were only held for a minimum of 11–12 hours prior to release, whereas in previous years fish were held for a minimum of 24 hours prior to being released over a 24-hour period. We also estimated survival for two additional releases in February 2010 conducted by the U.S. Army Corps of Engineers. These groups were released at the Elkhorn Boat ramp in the Sacramento River upstream of the Delta.

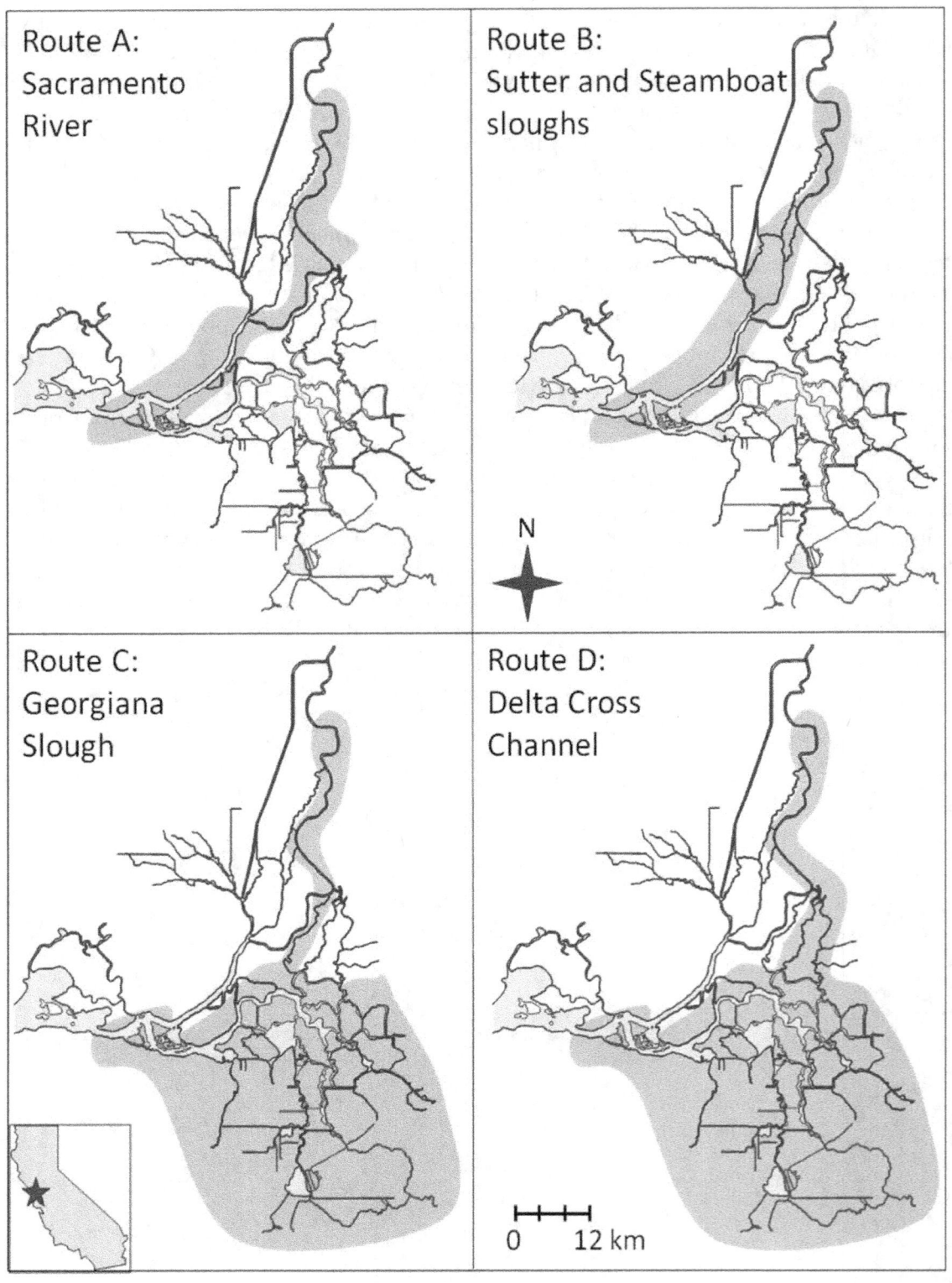

Figure 1. Maps of the Sacramento-San Joaquin River Delta with shaded regions showing river reaches that comprise survival through the Delta for four different migration routes. For routes C and D, the interior Delta is the large shaded region in the southernmost section of the migration route.

Methods

Telemetry System

Telemetry stations were deployed to monitor movement of tagged fish among four major migration routes through the Delta (fig. 1)—the mainstem Sacramento River (Route A), Steamboat and Sutter Sloughs (Route B), the interior Delta through the Delta Cross Channel (Route C), and the interior Delta through Georgiana Slough (Route D; fig. 1). Telemetry stations were labeled hierarchically to reflect the branching nature of channels at river junctions and their subsequent downstream convergence at the confluence of river channels (fig. 2). Each telemetry station consisted of single or multiple receivers (Vemco Ltd., Model VR2) that identified individual fish based on the unique pattern of acoustic pulses emitted from a transmitter. Because the Sacramento River is the primary migration route, the ith telemetry station within this route was denoted as A_i from the release site to the last telemetry station in the Delta at Chipps Island (A_9). Sutter and Steamboat Sloughs (labeled B_i) diverge from the Sacramento River at the first river junction and converge again with the Sacramento River upstream of A_7. We deployed numerous telemetry stations within Sutter and Steamboat Sloughs to quantify survival and movement within this region. Specifically, Sutter and Miner Sloughs form a northern route, and stations along this route are labeled B_{11} (entrance to Sutter Slough), B_{12}, and B_{13} (Miner Slough; fig. 2). A southern route is formed by Steamboat Slough, and these stations were labeled as B_{21}, B_{22}, and B_{23}. The entrance to the interior Delta through the Delta Cross Channel was labeled as C_1 where it diverges from the Sacramento River at the second river junction. Telemetry stations within Georgiana Slough and the interior Delta were labeled as D_i beginning where Georgiana Slough diverges from the mainstem Sacramento River at the second river junction (D_1) until the convergence of the interior Delta with the Sacramento River at D_7. Following this hierarchy, routes A, B, C, and D contained 8, 6, 1, and 7 telemetry stations. In addition, to quantify movement between the lower Sacramento River and the lower San Joaquin River, we included a telemetry station within Three Mile Slough (E_1) for a total of 23 telemetry stations within the Delta. Parameter subscripting and coding of detection histories followed this hierarchical structure (see section, "Model Development").

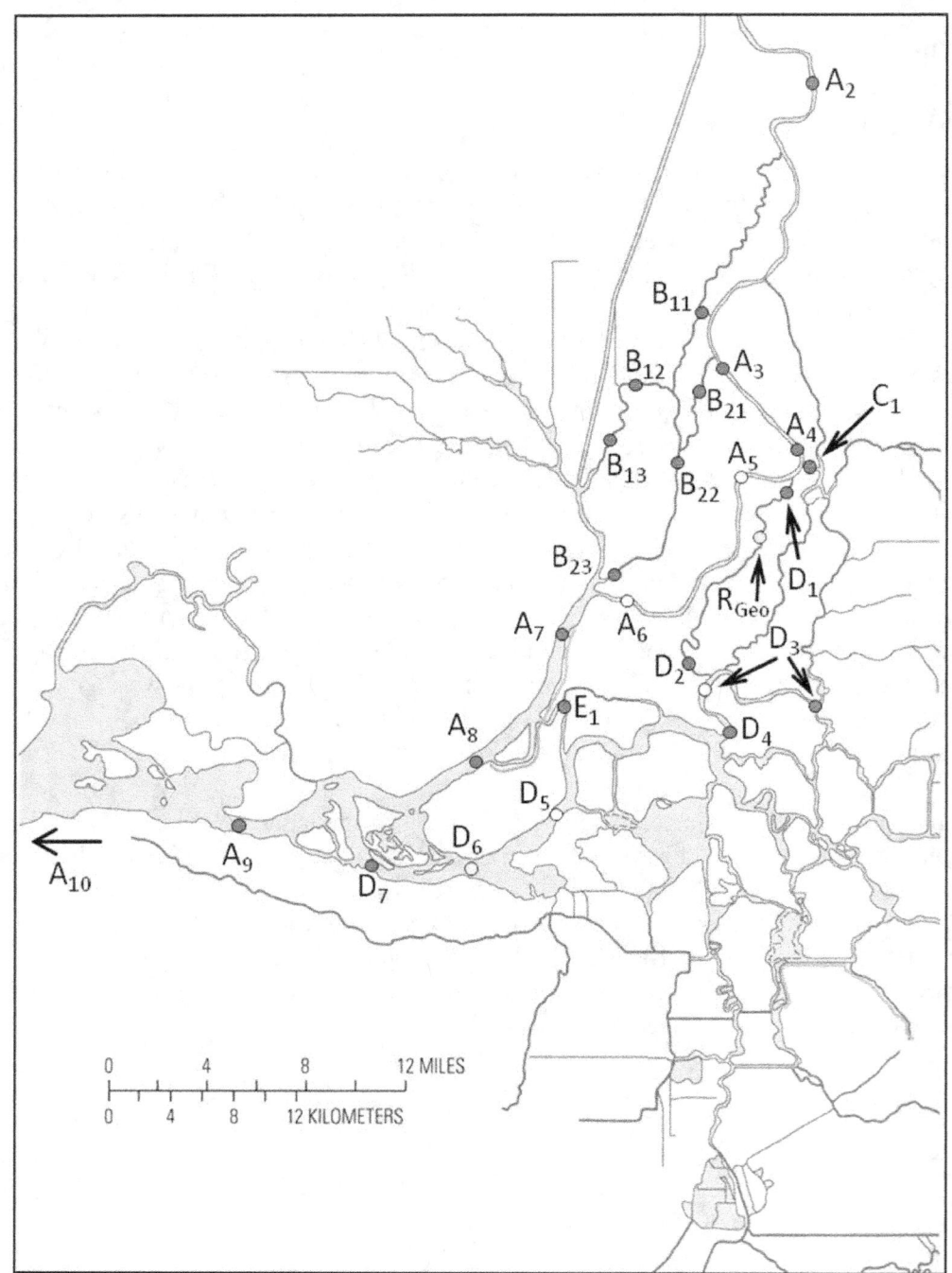

Figure 2. Map showing location of telemetry stations used to estimate survival and migration route probabilities within four major migration routes of the Sacramento-San Joaquin River Delta during the winter of 2009–10. Red-filled circles labeled as h_i show the location of telemetry station i with route h. Locations denoted by unfilled circles show telemetry stations used in 2007–08 but not 2009–10. Station A_{10} pools all telemetry stations in San Francisco Bay downstream of A_9. The Elkhorn Boat Ramp release site was 40 river kilometers upriver of station A_2, and the Georgiana release site is noted as the yellow-filled circle labeled as R_{Geo}.

With this configuration of telemetry stations, survival in the final reach (downstream of A_8 and D_7) is confounded with detection probability at the last telemetry station (Skalski and others, 2001). Therefore, to estimate survival to the terminus of the Delta, and detection probability at the last station in the Delta (A_9), we formed one additional telemetry station by pooling detections from numerous stations downstream of A_9 in San Francisco Bay (fig. 2). Most of these detections occurred at bridge-mounted telemetry stations that provided nearly complete cross-sectional coverage of San Francisco Bay, but single-monitor stations at other locations also were included.

Fish Tagging and Release

Juvenile late-fall Chinook salmon were obtained from the Coleman National Fish Hatchery (about 340 river kilometers upstream of the Elkhorn Boat Ramp near Sacramento). Fish were surgically implanted with a 1.6-g tag with a 70-d expected battery life (Vemco Ltd., Model V7-2L-R64K). Four releases were made at the Elkhorn Boat ramp, two in December 2009 (R_1 and R_2), one in January 2010 (R_3), and one in February 2010 (R_4). Hereafter, R_1 and R_2 are referred to as the December release groups, while R_3 and R_4 are referred to as the February release groups. The December releases were done on behalf of the U.S. Fish and Wildlife Service (USFWS), and the February releases were done on behalf of the U.S. Army Corps of Engineers (USACE; table 1).

For the December release groups, tags had a pulse delay of 20–60 s. Except for a minimum size criteria of 140-mm fork length, fish were randomly selected for tagging, resulting in a mean fork length (FL) of 153.3 mm (SD = 10.35) and mean weight of 41.1 g (SD = 9.4) for December releases. Fish were fasted for 24 h prior to surgery to ensure a post-absorptive state. To surgically implant transmitters, fish were anaesthetized using tricaine methanesulphonate (MS222). Once anesthetized, a small incision was made in the abdomen between the pectoral fins and the pelvic girdle. The transmitter was inserted into the peritoneal cavity, and the incision was closed with two interrupted sutures (4-0 nylon sutures with FS-2 cutting needle). After tagging was complete, fish were held for 24 hours before being transported to release sites at either the Sacramento River at Elkhorn Boat Ramp (40 km upstream of the Freeport station at A_2) or Georgiana Slough (about 5 km downstream of D_1; fig. 2). Tagged fish were then transferred to perforated 19-L buckets (two fish per bucket), held for 11–12 h at the release site to allow recovery from the transportation process, and then released every 4 hours at Sacramento and every 2 hours at Georgiana Slough. Each group was released over a 24-hour period to distribute release times over the tidal and diel cycle (table 1). Fish were released into Georgiana Slough 2 days after the Elkhorn release group to correlate release times in Georgiana Slough with the travel time of fish from Elkhorn Boat Ramp to Georgiana Slough.

For the February release groups, tags had a random pulse delay of 15–45 seconds. The tagged fish used for this release were obtained from the Coleman National Fish Hatchery and transported to University of California, Davis, where they were held prior to tagging. Fish used for this release had a mean fork length of 177.2 mm (SD=13.7) and a mean weight of 66.8 g (SD=29.4). Tagging procedures followed the same protocol as previously mentioned. Tagging was conducted over a 2-week period prior to release. Fish were then transported to Elkhorn Boat Ramp for release. Upon arrival at the release site, the river temperature was taken to ensure the fish were not stressed by a large temperature fluctuation, and the water was tempered accordingly. All fish were then released into the river after dark in order to provide refuge from predators within the first few hours of release.

Table 1. Summary of release dates, locations, and sample size of acoustically tagged late-fall Chinook salmon released into the Delta during the winter of 2009–10.

[Agency: USACE, U.S. Army Corps of Engineers; USFWS, U.S. Fish and Wildlife Service]

Agency	Release date	Release No.	Release location	Sample size
USFWS	December 2–3, 2009	1	Sacramento	167
USFWS	December 5, 2009	1	Georgiana Slough	72
USFWS	December 16–17, 2009	2	Sacramento	168
USFWS	December 19, 2009	2	Georgiana Slough	72
USACE	January 30, 2010	3	Sacramento	249
USACE	February 5, 2010	4	Sacramento	248

Model Development

We used the same survival model as the one developed for the 2008–09 migration year, presented in Perry and Skalski (2010). In this model, we estimated detection (P_{hi}), survival (S_{hi}), route entrainment probabilities (Ψ_{hl}), and joint survival-entrainment probabilities ($\phi_{hi,jk}$). Detection probabilities (P_{hi}) estimate the probability of detecting a transmitter assuming a fish is alive and the transmitter operational at telemetry station i within route h (h = A, B, C, D; fig. 2). Survival probabilities (S_{hi}) estimate the probability of surviving from telemetry station i to $i+1$ within route h (that is, to the next downstream telemetry station), conditional on surviving to station i (figs. 2 and 3). Route entrainment probabilities (Ψ_{hl}) estimate the probability of a fish entering route h at junction l (l = 1, 2), conditional on fish migrating through junction l (figs. 2 and 3). Joint survival-entrainment probabilities ($\phi_{hi,jk}$) estimate the joint probability of surviving from site h_i to j_k and moving into route j. The $\phi_{hi,jk}$ parameters are estimated in reaches with river junctions that split into two channels, but where telemetry stations within each river channel are located some distance downstream of the river junction. For example, fish passing station A_7 in the Sacramento River may enter Three Mile Slough (E_1) or remain in the Sacramento River for another 5.5 km downstream of this junction to pass station A_8 (fig. 2). Thus, $\phi_{hi,jk}$ is the joint probability of surviving from A_7 to its junction with Three Mile Slough, remaining in the Sacramento River at this junction, and then surviving from the junction to A_8.

For this study, telemetry stations within Sutter and Steamboat Sloughs downstream of each entrance allowed us to estimate route entrainment probabilities separately for each slough (figs. 2 and 3). The parameter Ψ_{B11} estimates the probability of being entrained into Sutter Slough at station B_{11}, and Ψ_{B21} estimates the probability of being entrained into Steamboat Slough at station B_{21}. Because route entrainment probabilities must sum to one at a given river junction, $1-\Psi_{B11}-\Psi_{B21} = \Psi_{A1}$ is the probability of remaining in the Sacramento River at the first junction (figs. 2 and 3).

As in previous years, the second junction was modeled as a three-branch junction where Ψ_{A2}, Ψ_{C2}, and $1-\Psi_{A2}-\Psi_{C2} = \Psi_{D2}$ estimate the probabilities of remaining in the Sacramento River (Route A), being entrained into the Delta Cross Channel (Route C), and entering Georgiana Slough (Route D) at junction 2 (figs. 2 and 3). However, a substantial fraction of the first release group passed the Delta Cross Channel after the gates had closed. Therefore, as with migration years 2007 and 2009 (Perry and others, 2010; Perry and Skalski, 2010), we incorporated a

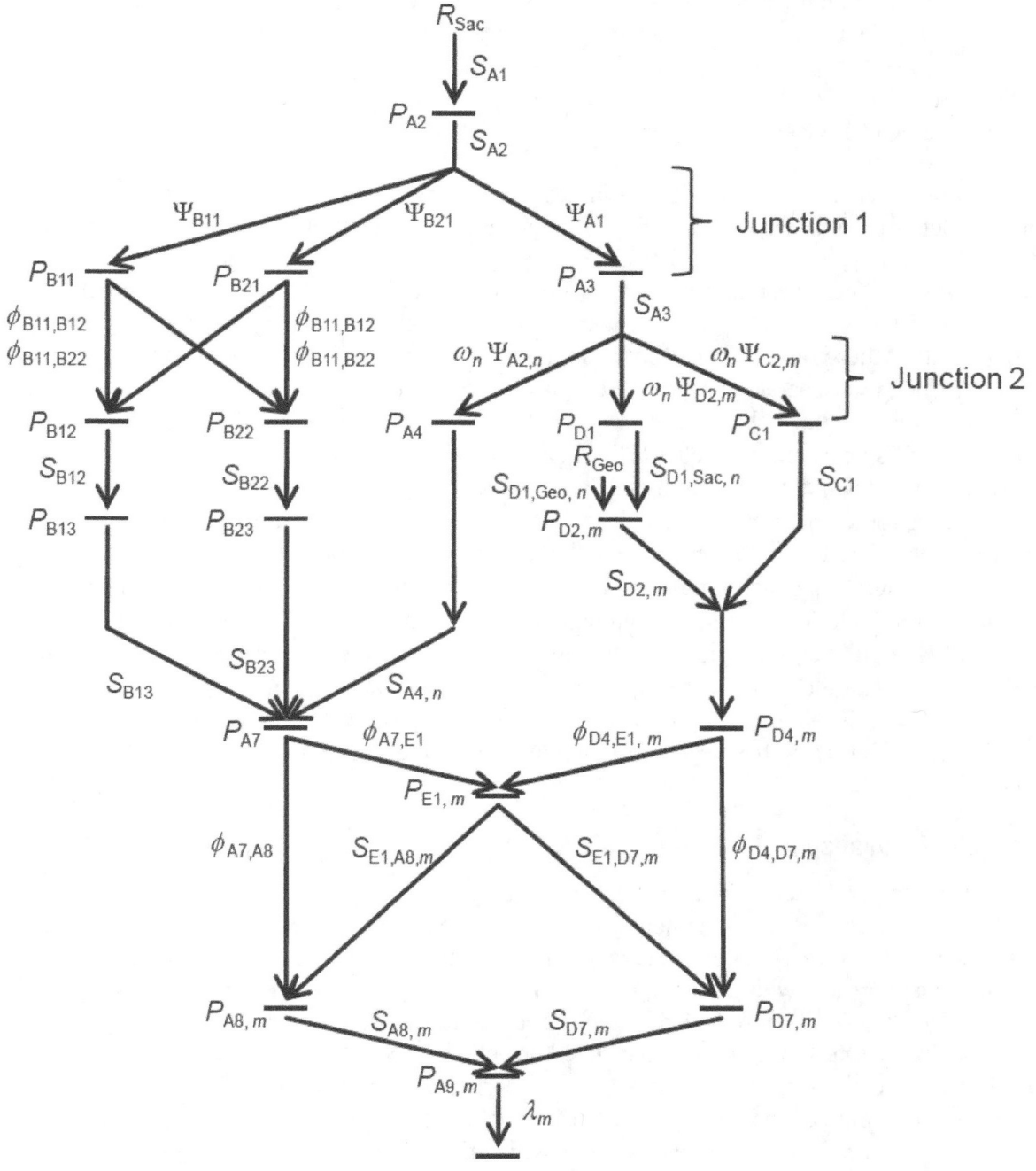

Figure 3. Schematic of the mark-recapture model used to estimate survival (S_{hi}), detection (P_{hi}), route entrainment (Ψ_{hi}), and joint survival-entrainment ($\phi_{hi,jk}$) probabilities of juvenile late-fall Chinook salmon migrating through the Sacramento–San Joaquin River Delta for releases made in winter of 2009–10. The parameter ω_n is the probability of passing the second river junction when the Delta Cross Channel was either open or closed. Release sites are denoted by R_m (m = Sac (Sacramento) and Geo (Georgiana Slough)), parameters subscripted by n are conditional on the position of the Delta Cross Channel gate, and m denote parameters which can be estimated separately for each release site.

parameter to estimate the probability of fish passing this river junction when the gates were open (ω_{open}, fig. 3). We then estimated route entrainment probabilities conditional on gate position (i.e., $\Psi_{hl,open}$ and $\Psi_{hl,closed}$). Route-specific survival was estimated for each release group. For the first release group, route-specific survival represents the average survival over conditions experienced by this release-group; that is, with the Delta Cross Channel gates both open and closed.

Joint survival-entrainment probabilities were estimated for three reaches where (1) fish entering Sutter Slough (B_{11}) or Steamboat Slough (B_{21}) may subsequently continue down either Miner Slough (B_{12}) or Steamboat Slough (B_{22}), (2) fish entering the San Joaquin River at D_4 may subsequently exit this reach through either Three Mile Slough at E_1 or the San Joaquin River at D_7, and (3) fish passing A_7 in the Sacramento River may exit this reach at either E_1 or A_8 (figs. 2 and 3). Each of these reaches consist of a single river channel, a junction where the channel splits, and then two separate channels through which fish migrate before being detected at telemetry stations in each channel. In these locations, interest may lie in estimating the proportion of fish entering each channel (that is, the route entrainment probabilities, Ψ_{hl}). However, when telemetry stations are located kilometers downstream of the river junction where fish enter one route or another, then estimates of Ψ_{hl} may be biased if survival probabilities downstream of the junction differ between the two channels. Despite this, estimates of the joint probability of surviving and migrating through a given channel (that is, $\phi_{hi,jk}$) will remain unbiased in these circumstances. Although the $\phi_{hi,jk}$ parameters are difficult to interpret biologically, being the joint probability of entrainment and survival, their sum yields the total reach survival. Therefore, in the reaches where $\phi_{hi,jk}$ parameters are estimated, $S_{B11} = \phi_{B11,B12} + \phi_{B11,B22}$, $S_{B21} = \phi_{B21,B12} + \phi_{B21,B22}$, $S_{A7} = \phi_{A7,E1} + \phi_{A7,A8}$, and $S_{D4} = \phi_{D4,E1} + \phi_{D4,D5}$ are the probabilities of surviving from each upstream telemetry station to either of the next downstream stations.

Parameter Estimation

Prior to parameter estimation, the records of tag detections were processed to eliminate false positive detections using methods based on Skalski and others (2002) and Pincock (2008). False positive detections of acoustic tags occur primarily when two or more tags are simultaneously present within the range of a given telemetry station, and simultaneous tag transmissions "collide" to produce a valid tag code that is not actually present at the monitor (Pincock, 2012). Our first criterion considered detections as valid if a minimum of two consecutive detections occurred within a 30-min period at a given telemetry station. Although this criterion minimized the probability of accepting a false positive detection, Pincock (2008) showed that a pair of false positive detections with a time interval less than 30 min occurred on average once every 30 days when simulating 10 tags simultaneously present at a monitor. Thus, our second criterion considered records with two detections at a given location as valid only if these detections were consistent with the spatiotemporal history of a tagged fish moving through the system of telemetry stations (Skalski and others, 2002). Detection records of fish that showed direct upstream movement over long distances against the flow were classified as predated fish. The detection records for 6 percent of fish showed evidence of predation, and were truncated to the hypothesized last known location of the live tagged fish. All other detections were considered to be live juvenile salmon. In the lower Sacramento and San Joaquin Rivers (sites A_7, A_8, and D_2), flows are tidally influenced, which can cause fish to move upstream during flood tides. To accommodate this behavior, the final downstream series of detections were used to form capture histories.

Detection histories compactly describe the migration and detection process of fish moving through the network of telemetry stations. For example, a fish with the history AA0AAAAEDDDAA indicates it was released at Sacramento ("A"), detected in the Sacramento River at A_2 ("A"), and not detected in the Sacramento River at A_3 ("0"). This fish was subsequently detected at every other telemetry station as it migrated from the Sacramento River ("AAAA") through Three Mile Slough ("E"), down the San Joaquin River ("DDD"), and finally past Chipps Island into San Francisco Bay ("AA"). Each detection history represents one cell of a multinomial distribution where the probability of each cell is defined as a function of the detection, survival, route entrainment, and joint survival-entrainment probabilities (see Perry and others, 2010, for an example). Given these cell probabilities, the maximum likelihood estimates are found by maximizing the likelihood function of a multinomial distribution with respect to the parameters:

$$L_{km}\left(\underset{\sim}{\beta}\middle| R_{km}, n_{jkm}\right) \propto \prod_{j=1}^{J} \pi_{jkm}^{n_{jkm}}, \tag{1}$$

where L_{km} is the likelihood for the kth release group ($k = 1, \ldots, 4$) at the mth release site [$m =$ Sacramento (Sac), Georgiana Slough (Geo)], R_{km} is the number of fish released for each release group and release site, n_{jkm} is the number of fish with the jth detection history in the kth release group at the mth release site, and π_{jkm} is the probability of the jth detection history in the kth release group at the mth release site expressed as a function of the parameters ($\underset{\sim}{\beta}$). The likelihood was numerically maximized with respect to the parameters using algorithms provided in the software program USER (Lady and others, 2008). Parameters were estimated separately for each release (k) but simultaneously for both release sites by expressing the joint likelihood as the product of $L_{k,\text{Sac}}$ and $L_{k,\text{Geo}}$. The variance-covariance matrix was estimated as the inverse of the Hessian matrix. We used the delta method (Seber, 1982) to estimate the variance of parameters that are functions of the maximum likelihood estimates. Uncertainty in parameter estimates is presented both as standard errors and 95-percent confidence intervals (that is, estimate ± 1.96*SE).

For each release, the full model was considered as the model with the fewest parameter constraints, which still allowed all parameters to be uniquely estimated. When parameter estimates occur at the boundaries of one (or zero), they cannot be estimated through iterative maximum likelihood techniques and must be set to one (or zero). In our study, many detection probabilities were set to one because all fish passing a given location were known to have been detected at that location. In some cases, survival probabilities were fixed to one because all fish detected at a given telemetry station also were detected at the next downstream location. In addition, parameters for Route C (the Delta Cross Channel) were set to zero when the Delta Cross Channel was closed. A full detailing of parameter constraints applied under the full model is provided in appendix A.

The purpose of including a separate release into Georgiana Slough was to improve precision of survival estimates within the interior Delta by increasing the sample size of fish migrating through this region. Pooling data across release sites can improve precision, but assumes that the fish released into the Sacramento River and Georgiana Slough experienced similar survival and detection probabilities in reaches through which both release groups migrated. Therefore, we used Akaike Information Criterion (AIC; Akaike, 1974) to evaluate hypotheses about equality in detection and survival parameters between release sites. For each release group, we compared the full model to a reduced model where all parameters were set equal between release sites. When AIC differed by greater than 2 between models, the model with lower AIC was selected as the most parsimonious model. We then used parameter estimates from the selected model for estimating population-level and route-specific survival through the Delta.

Survival through the Delta

Survival through the Delta is defined as the probability of survival from the entrance to the Delta at station A_2 (Freeport) to the exit of the Delta at station A_9 (Chipps Island). Population-level survival through the Delta was estimated from the individual components as:

$$S_{\text{Delta}} = \sum_{h=A}^{D} \Psi_h S_h ,$$ (2)

where S_h is the probability of surviving the Delta given the specific migration route taken through the Delta, and Ψ_h is the probability of migrating through the Delta via one of four migration routes (A = Sacramento River, B = Steamboat and Sutter Sloughs, C = Delta Cross Channel, D = Georgiana Slough). Thus, population survival through the Delta is a weighted average of the route-specific survival probabilities with weights equal to the fraction of fish migrating through each route.

Migration route probabilities are a function of the route entrainment probabilities at each of the two river junctions:

$$\Psi_A = \Psi_{A1}\Psi_{A2},$$ (3)

$$\Psi_B = \Psi_{B11} + \Psi_{B21},$$ (4)

$$\Psi_C = \Psi_{A1}\Psi_{C2}, \text{ and}$$ (5)

$$\Psi_D = \Psi_{A1}\Psi_{D2}.$$ (6)

For instance, consider a fish that migrates through the Delta via the Delta Cross Channel (Route C). To enter the Delta Cross Channel, this fish first remains in the Sacramento River at junction 1 with probability Ψ_{A1}, after which it enters the Delta Cross Channel at the second river junction with probability Ψ_{C2}. Thus, the probability of a fish migrating through the Delta through the Delta Cross Channel (Ψ_C) is the product of these route entrainment probabilities, $\Psi_{A1}\Psi_{C2}$.

When population level survival can be broken down into components of route-entrainment probabilities and reach specific survival, then survival through the Delta for a given migration route (S_h) is simply the product of the reach-specific survival probabilities that trace each migration path through the Delta between the points A_2 and A_9 (see Perry and others, 2010). However, when joint survival-entrainment probabilities are included in the model, survival through a given route must take into account all possible within-route pathways that involve the $\phi_{hi,jk}$ parameters. For example, survival through the Delta for fish that remain in the Sacramento River through the first and second river junctions is expressed as:

$$S_A = S_{A2}S_{A3}S_{A4}\left(\phi_{A7,A8}S_{A8} + \phi_{A7,E1}S_{E1,D7}S_{D7}\right).$$ (7)

The bracketed term is the weighted average survival between A_7 (Rio Vista) and A_9 (Chipps Island) with the $\phi_{hi,jk}$ parameters weighting survival of fish that remain in the Sacramento River and survival of fish that finish their migration in the lower San Joaquin River after passing through Three Mile Slough. Thus, Delta survival for Route A (the Sacramento River) includes some mortality of fish that enter the interior Delta, and it is impossible to factor out this mortality without explicitly estimating route entrainment probabilities at the junction of the Sacramento River with Three Mile Slough.

Survival through the Delta for fish taking the Delta Cross Channel (Route C) and Georgiana Slough (route D) is expressed similarly and explicitly accounts for fish that pass through Three Mile Slough and finish their migration in the lower Sacramento River:

$$S_C = S_{A2}S_{A3}S_{C1}\left(\phi_{D4,D7}S_{D7} + \phi_{D4,E1}S_{E1,A8}S_{A8}\right),\tag{8}$$

$$\text{and } S_D = S_{A2}S_{A3}S_{D1}S_{D2}\left(\phi_{D4,D7}S_{D7} + \phi_{D4,E1}S_{E1,A8}S_{A8}\right).\tag{9}$$

We pooled Sutter and Steamboat Sloughs into a single migration route, but survival through the Delta can be estimated separately for fish that enter Sutter Slough and fish that enter Steamboat Slough:

$$S_B = \Psi_{B11}S_{B1} + \Psi_{B21}S_{B2},\tag{10}$$

where S_B is survival through the Delta for fish that enter either Sutter or Steamboat Sloughs, S_{B1} and S_{B2} are survival through the Delta for fish that enter Sutter and Steamboat Sloughs, respectively, and where S_{B1} and S_{B2} are estimated as:

$$S_{B1} = S_{A2}\left(\phi_{B11,B12}S_{B12}S_{B13} + \phi_{B11,B22}S_{B22}S_{B23}\right)\left(\phi_{A7,A8}S_{A8} + \phi_{A7,E1}S_{E1,D7}S_{D7}\right),\tag{11}$$

$$\text{and } S_{B2} = S_{A2}\left(\phi_{B21,B12}S_{B12}S_{B13} + \phi_{B21,B22}S_{B22}S_{B23}\right)\left(\phi_{A7,A8}S_{A8} + \phi_{A7,E1}S_{E1,D7}S_{D7}\right).\tag{12}$$

Note that the first bracketed term in eqn. 9 and 10 accounts for survival of fish taking either Miner Slough ($S_{B12}S_{B13}$) or Steamboat Slough ($S_{B22}S_{B23}$) weighted by the joint probability of surviving and taking each of these routes ($\phi_{hi,jk}$).

We used an approach similar to Newman and Brandes (2001) to quantify survival through each migration route relative to survival of fish that migrate within the Sacramento River:

$$\theta_h = \frac{S_h}{S_A} \quad h \neq A.\tag{13}$$

We measured each route relative to route A because the Sacramento River is considered the primary migration route. For Georgiana Slough, θ_D is nearly analogous to θ estimated by Newman and Brandes (2001), who estimated the ratio of recovery rates of coded wire tagged fish released into Georgiana Slough and the Sacramento River near A_4. Survival through the Delta for route h is equal to Route A when $\theta_h = 1$, and survival through route h is less (greater) than Route A when θ_h is less (greater) than one. We interpreted survival through route h as significantly different than Route A at $\alpha = 0.05$ when $\theta_h = 1$ fell outside the 95-percent confidence interval of $\hat{\theta}_h$.

Results

River Conditions and Migration Timing

River conditions differed between the December and February release groups and influenced travel times of juvenile salmon through the Delta (fig. 4). For fish released in December, tagged fish passed the two river junctions when discharge of the Sacramento River at Freeport was about 10,000 ft³/s. In contrast, fish released in February migrated when discharge decreased from about 40,000 to 20,000 ft³/s, during the descending limb of a large freshet (fig. 4). These environmental conditions substantially influenced the travel times of juvenile salmon through the Delta.

The first release group took the longest to pass the second river junction (Stations A_4, C_1, and D_1 in fig. 2). The median travel time from release to this river junction was 16.8 d with an interquartile range (25th to 75th percentile) of 13.2–29.5 d ($n = 81$, fig. 4). The Delta Cross Channel was open at the time of release, but closed between 0955 on December 6 and 1001 on December 7. The Delta Cross Channel was then re-opened at 1002 on December 7, 2009, and closed again at 0958 hours on December 15, 2009, and remained closed for the balance of the study (fig. 4). Given the long travel times to this junction and the median arrival date of December 20, 2009, a substantial fraction of this release group passed the second river junction after Delta Cross Channel had closed (fig. 4).

The second release group traveled more quickly to river junction 2 compared to the first release group. Median travel times for R_2 (7.3 d, $n = 79$) were less than one-half that of R_1 (16.8 d, $n = 81$), and the interquartile range was narrower (3.5–11.7 d for R_1, 13.2–29.5 d for R_2; fig. 4). In addition, median travel time to Freeport (site A_2 in fig. 2), the first detection site in the Delta, was 14.8 d for R_1 ($n = 108$), but only 1.6 d for R_2 ($n = 124$), suggesting that the first release group delayed initiation of migration. Given that river discharge was similar for both release groups, these findings provide evidence that the first release group may not have been actively migrating smolts at the time of release.

Both February release groups (R_3 and R_4) traveled substantially faster to the second river junction than the December release groups (R_1 and R_2), probably due to higher discharge. Median travel times were 1.1 and 1.3 d for R_3 and R_4, with interquartile ranges of 0.98–1.2 d ($n = 55$) and 1.2–1.6 d ($n = 56$) for R_3 and R_4, respectively.

Due to higher river discharge in February, the February release groups also traveled more quickly to the exit of the Delta (Chipps Island) and had a more compressed travel time distribution (fig. 4). The December release groups had median travel times to Chipps Island of 30.1 d ($n = 47$) and 19.2 d ($n = 49$), respectively, for R_1 and R_2 (fig. 4). In contrast, median travel times for the February release groups were 6.2 d ($n = 105$) and 5.0 d ($n = 112$), respectively, for R_3 and R_4 (fig. 4).

Detection Probabilities

For the December release groups, as in past studies (Perry, 2010; Perry and others, 2010), detection probabilities at many telemetry stations were high (see appendix A, table A1). However, during high flows in February, detection probabilities in the upper Delta were considerably lower than previously observed (see appendix, table A1). For example, estimates of detection probabilities at Freeport, P_{A2}, were 1.0 for R_1 and R_2, and 0.823 for R_4, but only 0.18 for R_3, the group released during the highest river discharge. As another example, estimates of

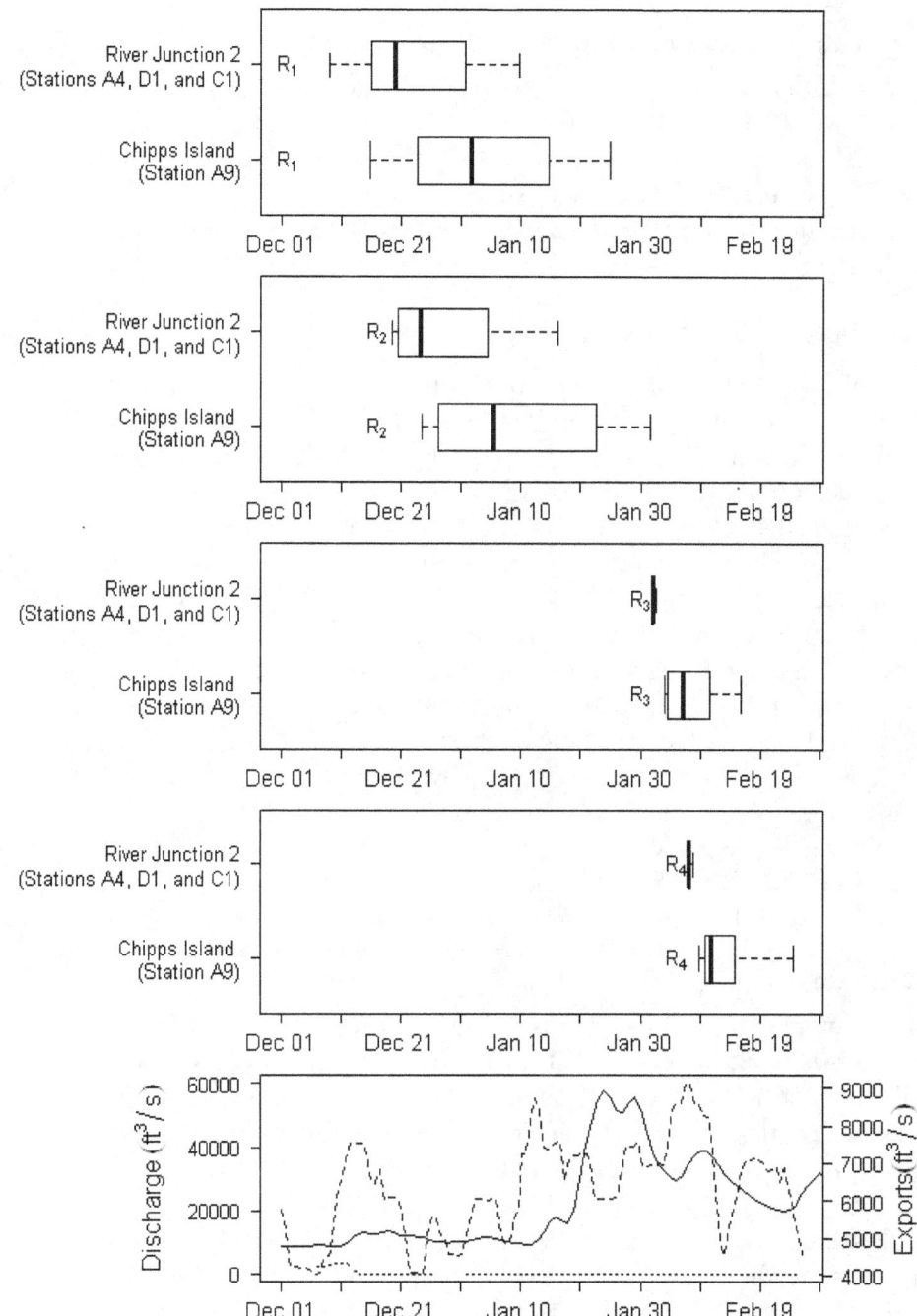

Figure 4. River discharge, water exports, and Delta Cross Channel discharge during the migration period of tagged juvenile Chinook salmon migrating through the Sacramento-San Joaquin River Delta during winter of 2009–10. Boxplots show the distribution of arrival dates at Junction 2 on the Sacramento River and at Chipps Island, the terminus of the Delta. The symbols R_1-R_4 are plotted at the release date. Whiskers represent the 10th and 90th percentiles, the box encompasses the 25th to 75th percentiles, and the line bisecting the box is the median arrival date. River discharge (solid line) is tidally filtered, daily discharge of the Sacramento River at Freeport (near telemetry station A_2), Delta Cross Channel discharge (dotted line) is the tidally filtered daily discharge, and water exports (dashed line) are the total daily discharge of water exported from the Delta at the pumping projects.

15

P_{A4} were 0.98, 0.99, 0.33, and 0.16 for R_1-R_4, respectively. These low detection probabilities influenced the precision of reach-specific survival estimates. For example, standard errors estimates for S_{A3} were 0.013, 0.031, 0.104, and 0.098 for R_1-R_4, respectively, despite larger sample sizes for R_3 and R_4 (appendix A, table A1). High flows likely caused tagged juvenile salmon to move very quickly past telemetry stations, causing low detection probabilities. The increased flow also may have decreased the effective detection range of receivers due to increased acoustic noise.

Route-Specific Survival through the Delta

Model selection criteria allowed us to pool parameters between release sites to improve precision of survival estimates. AIC for full model was 5.6 and 4.9 units larger than AIC for the reduced model, respectively for R_1 and R_2, suggesting no differences in survival or detection probabilities between Elkhorn Boat Ramp and Georgiana Slough release sites.

Compared to the differences in travel time, we found relatively little difference in survival through the Delta among release groups (table 2). Estimates of S_{Delta} ranged from 0.374 to 0.524 among release groups, a difference of 0.15 (table 2). However, differences in S_{Delta} among release groups were inconsistent with their travel times. For example, R_1 and R_3 exhibited similar survival through the Delta (table 2), but median travel times for R_1 were five times that of R_3 (fig. 2). Survival per day, expressed as a function of mean travel time from Freeport (station A_2) to Chipps Island (station A_9), was 0.949, 0.937, 0.881, and 0.920 for R_1–R_4, respectively, illustrating that survival rates per unit time were lower for the February release groups.

Patterns in route-specific survival were consistent across releases. Survival was highest for fish remaining in the Sacramento River and lowest for fish entering the interior Delta (fig. 5). As in previous years, survival for Sutter and Steamboat Sloughs combined was lower than for the Sacramento River for the December releases (R_1 and R_2), but was similar between these routes for the February releases (R_3 and R_4). Closer examination of this pattern revealed that survival of fish entering Steamboat Slough closely tracked survival for the Sacramento River; however, fish entering Sutter Slough exhibited lower survival than fish entering either Steamboat Slough or the Sacramento River (table 2, fig. 6). Furthermore, the difference in survival between Sutter and Steamboat Sloughs for the February release groups was less than the December release groups (table 2, fig. 6). These findings suggest that the increase in route specific survival for Sutter and Steamboat Sloughs for February release groups was driven by an increase in survival in Sutter Slough.

Cumulative survival as a function of distance traveled helps to compare differences in survival among migration routes and in different regions of the Delta (fig. 7). When mortality rate per unit distance traveled is constant, cumulative survival plotted on a log scale yields a straight line. However, slopes become more negative (that is, become steeper) moving from Freeport to Chipps Island, indicating that mortality rate per kilometer increases as fish transition from the upper to lower Delta (fig. 7). Specifically, the shallowest slopes (lowest mortality rates) occurred between Freeport (A_2) and the second river junction (A_4). Slopes become steeper in the tidal zone (A_4–A_9), indicating higher mortality rates per unit distance. Migration distances also vary among routes with Steamboat Slough being the shortest route to Chipps Island (67.4 km) and Georgiana Slough being the longest (94.1 km). Thus, if fish using different routes had the same mortality rate per unit distance, we would expect total survival to be lower for fish entering the interior Delta simply due to a longer migration distance. However, we observed the steepest slopes for fish entering the interior Delta, between station D_4 and A_9, indicating higher mortality

Table 2. Route-specific survival through the Sacramento–San Joaquin River Delta (S_h) and the probability of migrating through each route (Ψ_h) for acoustically tagged fall-run juvenile Chinook salmon released December 2–5, 2009 (R_1) and December 16–19, 2009 (R_2). Also shown is population survival through the Delta (S_{Delta}), which is the average of route-specific survival weighted by the probability of migrating through each route.

Migration route	S_h (SE)	95-percent confidence interval	Ψ_h (SE)	95-percent confidence interval
R_1: December 2-5, 2009				
A) Sacramento R.	0.584 (0.057)	0.472, 0.696	0.512 (0.048)	0.417, 0.606
B) Sutter & Steamboat S.	0.446 (0.076)	0.297, 0.595	0.223 (0.039)	0.146, 0.300
B_1) Sutter S.	0.336 (0.090)	0.159, 0.512	0.134 (0.032)	0.071, 0.197
B_2) Steamboat S.	0.612 (0.077)	0.461, 0.764	0.089 (0.027)	0.036, 0.142
C) Delta Cross Channel	0.236 (0.080)	0.080, 0.392	0.038 (0.019)	0.001, 0.074
D) Georgiana S.	0.248 (0.047)	0.156, 0.340	0.227 (0.041)	0.147, 0.307
S_{Delta} (All routes)	0.464 (0.044)	0.377, 0.551		
R_2: December 16-19, 2009				
A) Sacramento R.	0.510 (0.059)	0.395, 0.625	0.392 (0.045)	0.303, 0.481
B) Sutter & Steamboat S.	0.345 (0.061)	0.225, 0.465	0.319 (0.043)	0.234, 0.404
B_1) Sutter S.	0.302 (0.065)	0.176, 0.429	0.243 (0.044)	0.158, 0.328
B_2) Steamboat S.	0.483 (0.087)	0.312, 0.653	0.076 (0.028)	0.020, 0.131
C) Delta Cross Channel	NA	NA	0.000 (0.000)	NA
D) Georgiana S.	0.223 (0.040)	0.144, 0.301	0.289 (0.042)	0.207, 0.371
S_{Delta} (All routes)	0.374 (0.040)	0.296, 0.452		
R_3: January 31, 2010				
A) Sacramento R.	0.485 (0.059)	0.371, 0.600	0.449 (0.045)	0.361, 0.537
B) Sutter & Steamboat S.	0.468 (0.062)	0.347, 0.589	0.447 (0.049)	0.352, 0.542
B_1) Sutter S.	0.432 (0.079)	0.276, 0.588	0.242 (0.091)	0.063, 0.420
B_2) Steamboat S.	0.510 (0.084)	0.346, 0.675	0.205 (0.085)	0.038, 0.372
C) Delta Cross Channel	NA	NA	0.000 (0.000)	NA
D) Georgiana S.	0.179 (0.074)	0.034, 0.324	0.104 (0.022)	0.061, 0.148
S_{Delta} (All routes)	0.446 (0.041)	0.365, 0.526		
R_4: February 5, 2010				
A) Sacramento R.	0.577 (0.043)	0.492, 0.662	0.600 (0.038)	0.526, 0.673
B) Sutter & Steamboat S.	0.550 (0.061)	0.430, 0.669	0.221 (0.030)	0.162, 0.279
B_1) Sutter S.	0.508 (0.076)	0.359, 0.657	0.135 (0.027)	0.082, 0.188
B_2) Steamboat S.	0.616 (0.071)	0.476, 0.755	0.086 (0.022)	0.044, 0.128
C) Delta Cross Channel	NA	NA	0.000 (0.000)	NA
D) Georgiana S.	0.314 (0.075)	0.167, 0.461	0.179 (0.030)	0.120, 0.239
S_{Delta} (All routes)	0.524 (0.034)	0.457, 0.591		

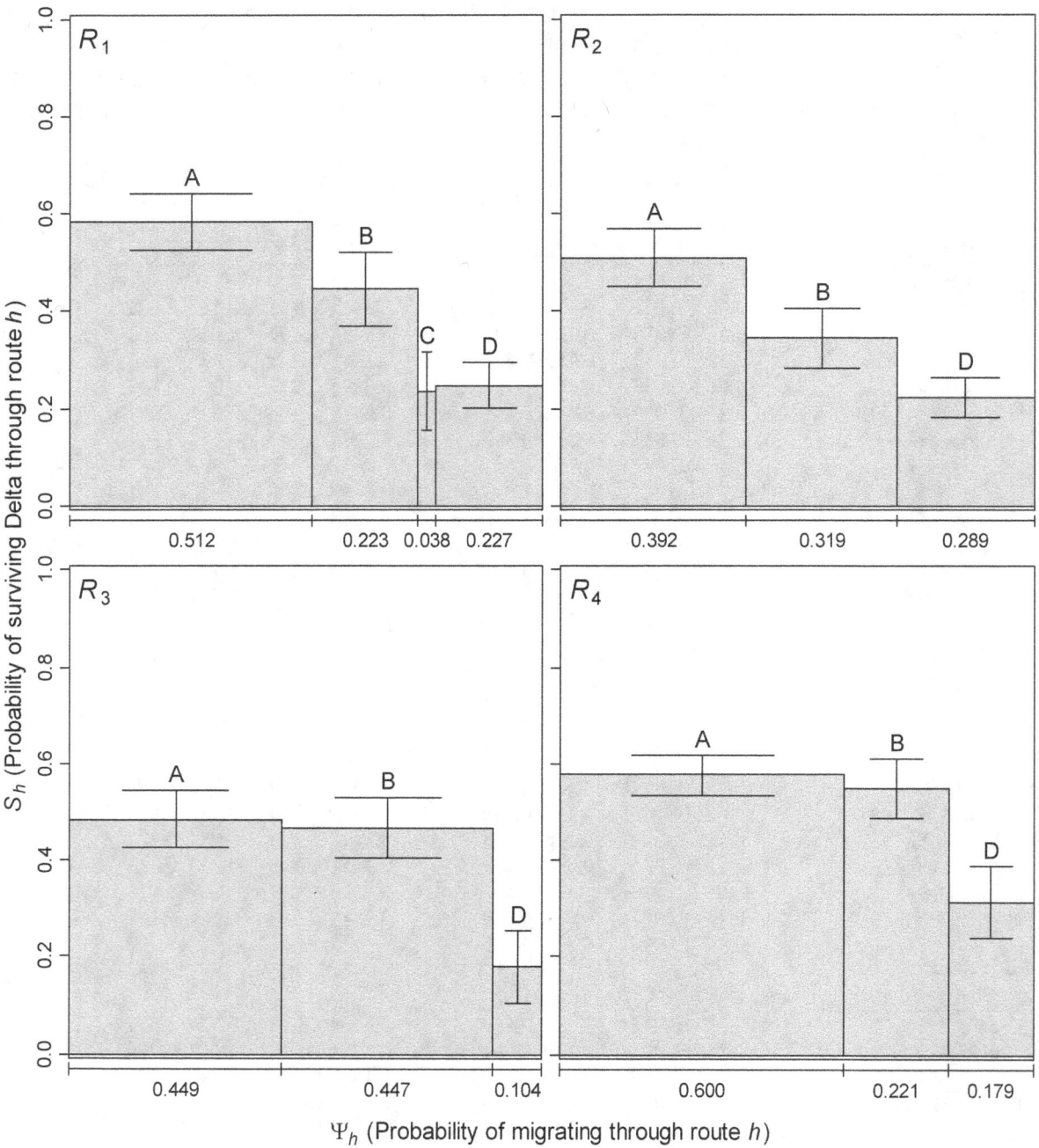

Figure 5. Probability of surviving migration through the Sacramento-San Joaquin River Delta (S_h) for each of four migration routes for tagged late-fall juvenile Chinook salmon migrating from the Sacramento River. The width of each bar shows the fraction of fish migrating through each route (Ψ_h), and the total area under the bars yields S_{Delta}. Labels A–D represent the Sacramento River, Steamboat and Sutter Sloughs, the Delta Cross Channel, and Georgiana Slough, respectively.

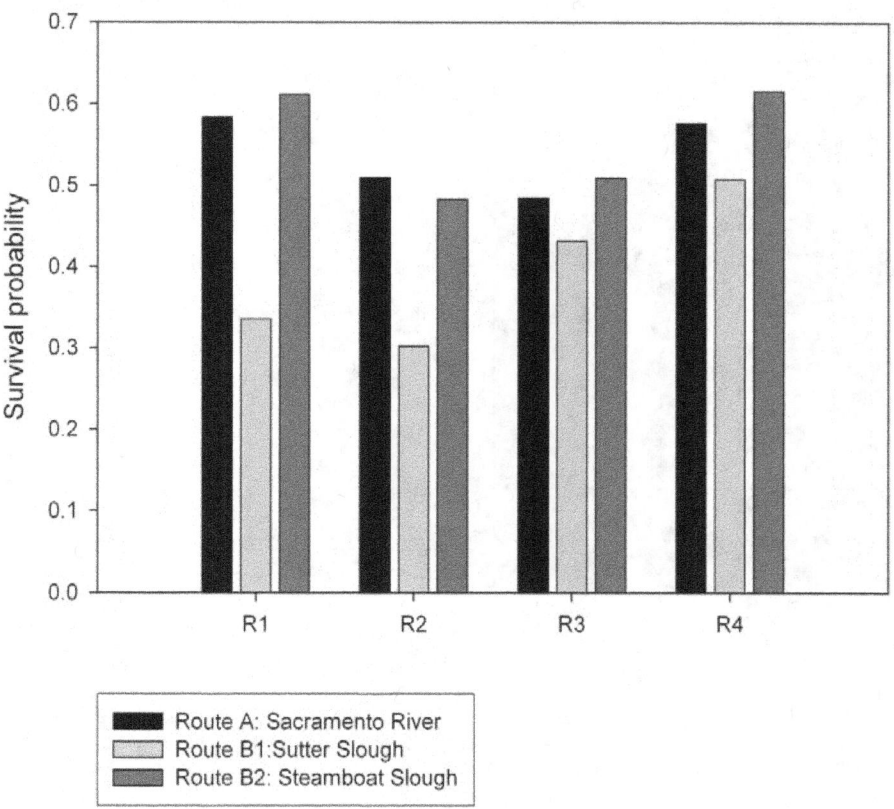

Figure 6. Comparison of route-specific survival between the Sacramento River (A), Sutter Slough (B_1), and Steamboat Slough (B_2) for late-fall Chinook salmon tagged and released in December 2009 (R_1 and R_2) and February 2010 (R_3 and R_4).

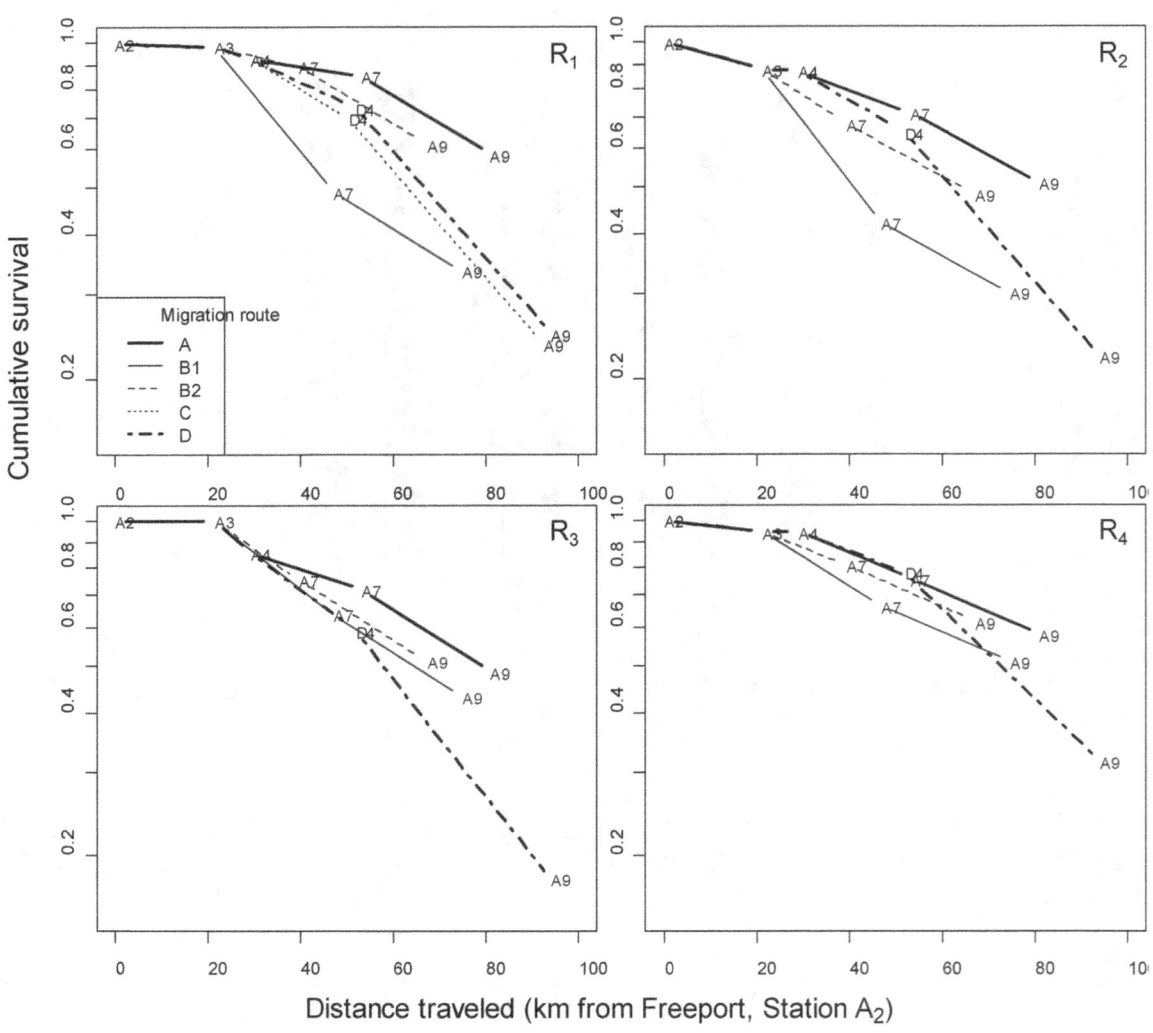

Figure 7. Cumulative survival for each migration route as a function of distance traveled for juvenile late-fall Chinook salmon released in December 2009 (R_1 and R_2) and February 2010 (R_3 and R_4). Symbols show cumulative survival to each telemetry station (A2 = Freeport and A9 = Chipps Island; see fig. 2 for others) for fish traversing different migration routes (A = Sacramento River, B1 = Sutter Slough, B2 = Steamboat Slough, C = Delta Cross Channel, D = Georgiana Slough). Distance traveled was calculated using the shortest pathway within each migration route. Note that the y-axis is plotted on a log scale. Common slopes on a log scale indicate equal mortality rates per unit distance traveled.

per unit distance than other routes (fig. 7). Taken together, the higher rate of mortality per unit distance and the longer distance traveled through the interior Delta acts to reduce survival considerably compared to other migration routes.

Differences in survival expressed as the ratio of survival for each major migration route relative to the Sacramento River (that is, θ_h) supported conclusions based on comparison of survival between routes (table 3). For fish entering the interior Delta through the Delta Cross Channel or Georgiana Slough, $\theta_h = 1$ fell outside the 95-percent confidence intervals for all releases, supporting the hypothesis that fish entering the interior Delta had significantly lower survival than fish entering the Sacramento River (table 3). The combined survival of fish entering Sutter and Steamboat Sloughs was significantly lower than the Sacramento River only for R_2. However, when Sutter and Steamboat Sloughs were analyzed independently of each other, θ_{B2} for Steamboat Slough was not significantly different from 1.0 for all releases. In contrast, θ_{B1} for Sutter Slough was significantly different from 1.0 for the December releases, but not for the February releases.

Table 3. Ratio (θ_h) of survival through route h (S_h) to survival through the Sacramento River (S_A) for acoustically tagged late fall-run juvenile Chinook salmon released in December 2–5 and December 16–19, 2009.

Migration route	θ_h (SE)	95-percent confidence interval	θ_h (SE)	95-percent confidence interval
	R_1: December 2-5		R_2: December 16-19	
B) Sutter & Sutter S.	0.765 (0.122)	0.525, 1.004	0.677 (0.119)	0.443, 0.911
B1) Sutter S.	0.575 (0.150)	0.281, 0.869	0.593 (0.126)	0.346, 0.840
B2) Steamboat S.	1.049 (0.117)	0.820, 1.278	0.948 (0.168)	0.619, 1.276
C) Delta Cross Channel	0.404 (0.140)	0.130, 0.679	NA	NA
D) Georgiana S.	0.425 (0.087)	0.255, 0.595	0.437 (0.087)	0.266, 0.607
	R_3: January 30		R_4: February 5	
B) Sutter & Sutter S.	0.964 (0.168)	0.635, 1.292	0.952 (0.114)	0.728, 1.176
B_1) Sutter S.	0.890 (0.195)	0.507, 1.272	0.880 (0.139)	0.608, 1.152
B_2) Steamboat S.	1.051 (0.202)	0.656, 1.447	1.066 (0.129)	0.813, 1.319
C) Delta Cross Channel	NA	NA	NA	NA
D) Georgiana S.	0.369 (0.151)	0.073, 0.664	0.545 (0.139)	0.272, 0.817

Migration Routing

Migration routing varied considerably among release groups. The Delta Cross Channel was closed for all release groups except R_1, and only 3.8 percent of this release group entered the Delta Cross Channel. However, due to long travel times, only 18.5 percent of this release group passed the Delta Cross Channel while the gates were open (table 4). Of the fish that passed the Delta Cross Channel while the gates were open, 20 percent entered the Delta Cross Channel, which is consistent with previous studies (table 4).

Table 4. Probability of migrating through each route (Ψ_h) for acoustically tagged late fall-run juvenile Chinook salmon released in December 2009 as a function of gate position when fish passed the Delta Cross Channel.

[Only 18.5 percent of fish passed the cross channel when it was open ($\omega_{open} = 0.185$, SE = 0.043)]

Migration route	Cross channel open		Cross channel closed	
	Ψ_h (SE)	95-percent confidence interval	Ψ_h (SE)	95-percent confidence interval
A) Sacramento R.	0.521 (0.097)	0.330, 0.713	0.510 (0.052)	0.408, 0.612
B) Sutter & Steamboat S.	0.223 (0.039)	0.146, 0.300	0.223 (0.039)	0.146, 0.300
C) Delta Cross Channel	0.204 (0.088)	0.031, 0.378	NA	
D) Georgiana S.	0.051 (0.049)	-0.046, 0.148	0.267 (0.047)	0.195, 0.348

The fraction of fish entering the interior Delta for the December releases, during low flows, was higher than for the February releases. Routing probabilities for Sutter and Steamboat Sloughs affect the proportion of fish entering the interior Delta because fish entering Sutter and Steamboat Sloughs bypass the entrance to the interior Delta. For example, R_3 exhibited the highest fraction of fish entering Sutter and Steamboat Sloughs (45 percent) and consequently the lowest fraction entering the interior Delta (10.4 percent) because only about one-half of this release group remained in the Sacramento River. Route entrainment probabilities at the second river junction also influence the fraction of the population entering the interior Delta. For example, of the fish that arrive at Georgiana Slough with the Delta Cross Channel closed, 34.4, 42.5, 18.8, and 23.0 percent, entered the interior Delta, respectively, for R_1-R_4 (see $\Psi_{D2,closed}$ in the appendix A, table A1). These findings show that entrainment into the interior Delta is higher during low flow, a finding consistent with Perry (2010).

Entrainment into Sutter and Steamboat Sloughs varied considerably among releases ranging from 22.1 percent for R_2 to 44.7 percent for R_3. The majority of fish taking this route entered Sutter Slough. Migration route probabilities for Sutter Slough ranged from 13.4 to 24.3 percent among releases. In contrast, entrainment into Steamboat Slough was 7.6–8.9 percent, except for R_3 when 20.5 percent entered Steamboat Slough.

Relative Contributions to S_{Delta}

The fraction of fish using each migration route combined with route-specific survival influenced overall survival through the Delta. For example, R_2 exhibited the lowest S_{Delta} among release groups (0.374) and lowest fraction of fish remaining in the Sacramento River. Because the Sacramento River had the highest survival for R_1 and R_2, reducing the fraction remaining in the Sacramento River acts to reduce overall survival through the Delta. For R_3 and R_4, fish entering the interior Delta had considerably lower survival than either the Sacramento River or Sutter and Steamboat Sloughs. However, less than 20 percent of fish entered the interior Delta resulting in a low contribution of this route to S_{Delta}.

Discussion

This report presents the fourth year of route-specific survival of late-fall Chinook salmon; some findings were similar to previous years, but others were contrary to previous findings. Similar findings to previous years include: (1) highest Chinook salmon survival in the Sacramento River, and lowest survival for routes leading to the interior Delta, (2) Chinook salmon survival in Sutter and Steamboat Sloughs lower than that of the Sacramento River during December releases, but similar during later releases, and (3) similar patterns of Chinook salmon migration routing among years. Findings that differed from previous years include: (1) delayed migration for fish released in early December, (2) less-than-expected differences in Chinook salmon survival between release groups relative to the differences in river flows experienced by each release group, and (3) low detection probabilities for some telemetry stations during the high flows of the February 2010 release groups.

During the 2010 migration year, Chinook salmon survival in the Sacramento River was higher than for the migration routes leading to the interior Delta. This finding is particularly important given that 2010 was the first year in which some release groups migrated wholly during relatively higher river flows. In the previous 3 years, most fish migrated during the lower range of Sacramento River flows. Flows during previous years averaged about 10,000 ft³/s at Freeport, whereas the February 2010 release group experienced flows ranging from 20,000 to 40,000 ft³/s at Freeport. Even under the higher flows experienced by this release group, we observed lower survival for the interior Delta than the Sacramento River. In addition, ratios of survival between these routes were similar among release groups ranging from 0.369 to 0.545 (table 3). These findings suggest that differences in survival between these migration routes exist over a range of flows.

Although patterns in survival differences among routes remained consistent across years, we might have expected a larger difference in survival probabilities relative to the flows and travel time differences among release groups. Perry (2010) found that route-specific survival for the Sacramento River and Sutter and Steamboat Sloughs was positively correlated to both fish size and flow of the Sacramento River. The February release groups were comprised of larger fish, migrated during higher flows, and had shorter travel times than the December release groups. Given the findings of Perry (2010), we would expect to observe a larger difference in survival between release groups, but this was not the case. Differences in travel times suggest that the February release group experienced lower survival rates when expressed as survival per unit time. A number of factors may have been at play in determining observed survival. One potential mechanism is the underlying differences in the study population of fish used during the December releases relative to the February releases. Our previous analyses, and the December release group of this study, were comprised of fish tagged at Coleman National Fish Hatchery. This population closely matches the rearing and holding conditions experienced by the untagged hatchery population. In contrast, fish used for the February release group were transported to U.C. Davis and reared under different conditions than the general population of fish at Coleman National Fish Hatchery. The February release group was held at U.C. Davis for up to 2 weeks following tagging before being transported to the release site. Release protocols also differed between release groups. The December release group was released at 4-hour intervals over a 24-hour period in order to distribute fish over the tidal and diel cycle, whereas the February release group was entirely released at night in a single batch. Thus, in addition to being substantially larger, differences in rearing history and release pattern may have introduced variation in survival among release groups. Last seasonal differences other than flow (for example, predator densities) may account for differences in survival among release groups.

Examining cumulative survival provided insights into the manner in which migration distance and mortality per unit distance interact to affect total survival for each migration route. For fish migrating through the interior Delta, which is the longest migration route, we found that mortality rate per unit distance was higher than other routes. One way of interpreting this finding is that survival through the interior Delta would be lower than other routes, even if migration distance was the same among routes. Alternatively, if mortality rates per unit distance had been the same among routes, survival through the interior Delta would be lower due to a longer migration distance. Higher mortality per unit distance combined with longer migration distance provides one mechanism for explaining the consistently lower survival for fish entering the interior Delta relative to the Sacramento River.

The pattern of cumulative survival with respect to distance also is consistent with the predator encounter rate model proposed by Anderson and others (2005). Under this model, when prey migrate through a "gauntlet" of predators, predator-prey encounter rates will be such that each prey encounters a predator one time at most. Under these circumstances, predator-prey theory predicts that survival will be driven by distance traveled, but not by travel time. In contrast, when prey migration speeds are slow relative to predator swimming speeds such that multiple encounters are possible, then the situation reverses: the probability of survival becomes dependent on travel time. This hypothesis is consistent with the steepening slope between cumulative survival and distance traveled as fish transition from the upper to lower Delta (fig. 7). Within our study area, the Sacramento River transitions from river-driven discharge in the uppermost reaches to tidally driven discharge in the lower reaches. Coincident with this transition, fish movement patterns shift from downstream-only movements to both upstream and downstream movements in the lower reaches of the Delta. Thus, in lower reaches of the Delta, fish may pass through a given reach more than once. This process could increase predator encounter rates relative to the length of each reach, therefore increasing mortality rates per unit distance.

The high flows during the third and fourth releases probably caused low detection probabilities relative to the first two releases. Low detection probabilities occurred because of a combination of the tag design and the proofing algorithm. At high flows, it is possible for a fish to be moving at such speeds that the tag "pulses" zero or one time while in the detection zone of a hydrophone. For example, we observed numerous fish with only a single detection at a hydrophone, which fails our criterion for a valid detection event (a minimum of two detections). Although many of these detections may have been valid, relaxing this criterion increases the risk of accepting false positive detections. Because including false positive detection introduces bias into survival estimates, we elected to maintain our criterion at a minimum of two detections. Low detection probabilities suggest that the pulse rates of these transmitters may have been too slow for the high river flows and water velocities observed in February 2010. Future studies should consider reducing the pulse rate to increase detection probabilities during high flows. Instream acoustic noise also may have contributed to the low detections probabilities. Increased flows often decrease detection range of VR2 receivers. The release strategy also may have affected tag detection for the February group. Given the number of tagged fish released in a single batch, it is possible that tag collisions occurred at telemetry stations first encountered by fish. For tags to be detected, fish would have to be within receiver range a greater period of time to account for the tag signals potentially canceling each other out.

We observed that entrainment probabilities for routes leading to the interior Delta (Ψ_{C2} and Ψ_{D2}, table A1 in appendix A) were lower during the high flows experienced by the February release groups, which is consistent with an inverse relationship between flow and entrainment probability at this river junction. Perry (2010) found that daily entrainment probabilities decreased as the proportion of river flow entering the interior Delta increased. In turn, the fraction of discharge entering the interior Delta increases as flow decreases. Because a lower fraction of the population entered the interior Delta during February releases, this route contributed less to S_{Delta} relative to December release groups, thereby increasing overall survival through the Delta. For example, had migration route probabilities for the interior Delta for R_3 ($\Psi_D = 0.104$) been similar to R_2 ($\Psi_D = 0.289$), S_{Delta} would have been 0.390 instead of 0.445. This example illustrates the interplay between migration routing and overall survival in the Delta.

Determining which factors influence the migration and survival dynamics of juvenile Chinook salmon is critical to the management and recovery of salmon in the Central Valley. After 4 years of study, patterns in survival and movement dynamics are beginning to emerge. Such information helps to inform management actions that will improve survival of juvenile salmonid populations migrating through the Sacramento-San Joaquin River Delta.

Acknowledgments

Tagging of juvenile salmon, ultrasonic station deployment and interrogation, and tag-detection database maintenance were supported by a grant from the California Bay-Delta Authority by Agreement No. U-05-SC-047 (A. Peter Klimley and Bruce MacFarlane, PIs). We thank Kevin Niemela, Kurtis Brown, and Scott Hamelburg of U.S. Fish and Wildlife Service and the staff of Coleman National Fish Hatchery for providing the late-fall Chinook and logistical support at the hatchery for this study. We are grateful to the following staff of the U.S. Fish and Wildlife Service in Stockton, California, for assisting with transport, holding, and release of tagged fish: Phil Voong, Dustin Dinh, Denise Barnard, Amber Aguilera, Pete Hrodey, Mike Marshall, Amy Combs and Patricia Brandes. Lynne Casal, USGS, was instrumental in assisting with report construction and formatting.

References Cited

Akaike, H., 1974, A new look at the statistical model identification: IEEE Transactions on Automatic control, v. 19, p. 716–723.

Anderson, J.J., Gurarie, E., and Zabel, R.W., 2005, Mean free-path length theory of predator-prey interactions—Application to juvenile salmon migration: Ecological modeling, v. 186, p. 196–211.

Baker, P.F., and Morhardt, J.E., 2001, Survival of Chinook salmon smolts in the Sacramento-San Joaquin Delta and Pacific Ocean, *in* Brown, R.L., ed., Contributions to the Biology of Central Valley Salmonids: Sacramento, California Department of Fish and Game, Fish Bulletin 179, v. 2, p. 163–182.

Brandes, P.L., and McLain, J.S., 2001, Juvenile Chinook salmon abundance, distribution, and survival in the Sacramento-San Joaquin Estuary, *in* Brown, R.L., ed., Contributions to the Biology of Central Valley Salmonids: Sacramento, California Department of Fish and Game, Fish Bulletin 179, v. 2, p. 39–138.

Kimmerer, W.J., 2008, Losses of Sacramento River Chinook salmon and delta smelt to entrainment in water diversions in the Sacramento-San Joaquin Delta: San Francisco Estuary and Watershed Science, v. 6, no. 2, p. 1–27.

Kjelson, M.A., Raquel, P.F., and Fisher, F.W., 1981, Influences of freshwater inflow on Chinook salmon (*Oncorhynchus tshawytscha*) in the Sacramento-San Joaquin Estuary, *in* Cross, R.D., and Williams, D.L., eds., Proceedings of the National Symposium Freshwater inflow to Estuaries: U.S. Fish and Wildlife Service, FWS/OBS-81/04, v. 2, p. 88–108.

Lady, J.M., Westhagen, P., and Skalski, J.R., 2008, USER 4—User-specified estimation routine: School of Aquatic and Fishery Sciences, University of Washington, accessed August 13, 2012, at http://www.cbr.washington.edu/paramest/user/.

Myers, J.M., Kope, R.G., Bryant, G.J., Teel, D., Lierheimer, L.J., Wainwright, T.C., Grant, W.S., Waknitz, F.W., Neely, K., Lindley, S.T., and Waples, R.S., 1998, Status review of Chinook salmon from Washington, Idaho, Oregon, and California: National Oceanic and Atmospheric Administration, NOAA Technical Memorandum, NFMS-NWFSC-35.

National Marine Fisheries Service, 1997, National Marine Fisheries Service proposed recovery plan for the Sacramento River winter-run Chinook: Long Beach, California, National Marine Fisheries Service, Southwest Regional Office, 8 p.

National Oceanic and Atmospheric Administration, 2008, Fisheries off West Coast States and in the Western Pacific—West Coast salmon fisheries—2008 management measures and a temporary rule: Federal Register, v. 73, p. 23,971–23,981.

Nehlsen, W., Williams, J.E., and Lichatowich, J.A., 1991, Pacific salmon at the crossroads—Stocks at risk from California, Oregon, Idaho, and Washington: Fisheries, v. 16, no. 2, p. 4–21.

Newman, K.B., 2003, Modeling paired release-recovery data in the presence of survival and capture heterogeneity with application to marked juvenile salmon: Statistical Modeling, v. 3, p. 157–177.

Newman, K.B., 2008, An evaluation of four Sacramento-San Joaquin River Delta juvenile salmon survival studies: Stockton, California, U.S. Fish and Wildlife Service, Project number SCI-06-G06-299, accessed August 13, 2012, at http://www.science.calwater.ca.gov/pdf/psp/PSP_2004_final/PSP_CalFed_FWS_salmon_studi es_final_033108.pdf.

Newman, K.B., and Brandes, P.L., 2010, Hierarchical modeling of juvenile Chinook salmon survival as a function of Sacramento-San Joaquin Delta water exports: North American Journal of Fisheries Management, v. 30, p. 157–169.

Newman, K.B., and Rice, J., 2002, Modeling the survival of Chinook salmon smolts outmigrating through the lower Sacramento River system: Journal of the American Statistical Association, v. 97, p. 983–993.

Nichols, F.H., Cloern, J.E., Luoma, S.N., and Peterson, D.H., 1986, The modification of an estuary: Science, v. 4,738, p. 567–573.

Perry, R.W., 2010, Survival and migration dynamics of juvenile Chinook salmon (*Oncorhynchus tshawytscha*) in the Sacramento-San Joaquin River Delta: Seattle, University of Washington, Pd.D. dissertation, 223 p.

Perry, R.W., and Skalski, J.R., 2010, Individual-, release-, and route-specific variation in survival of juvenile Chinook salmon migrating through the Sacramento-San Joaquin River Delta: Stockton, California, Report to U.S. Fish and Wildlife Services, 47 p.

Perry, R.W., Skalski, J.R., Brandes, P.L., Sandstrom, P.T., Klimley, A.P., Ammann, A., and MacFarlane, B., 2010, Estimating survival and migration route probabilities of juvenile Chinook salmon in the Sacramento-San Joaquin River Delta: North American Journal of Fisheries Management, v. 30, p. 142–156.

Pincock, D.G., 2008, False detections—What they are and how to remove them from detection data: VEMCO division of AMIRIX Systems, Inc., accessed August 13, 2012, at http://www.vemco.com/pdf/false_detections.pdf.

Seber, G.A.F., 1982, The estimation of animal abundance and related parameters (2d ed.): Caldwell, N.J., Blackburn Press, 654 p.

Skalski, J.R., Lady, J., Townsend, R., Giorgi, A.E., Stevenson, J.R., Peven, C.M., and McDonald, R.D., 2001, Estimating in-river survival of migrating salmonid smolts using radiotelemetry: Canadian Journal of Fisheries and Aquatic Sciences, v. 58, p. 1,987–1,997.

Skalski, J.R., Townsend, R., Lady, J., Giorgi, A.E., Stevenson, J.R., and McDonald, R.D., 2002, Estimating route-specific passage and survival probabilities at a hydroelectric project from smolt radiotelemetry studies: Canadian Journal of Fisheries and Aquatic Sciences, v. 59, p. 1,385–1,393.

Williams, J.G., 2006, Central Valley salmon—A perspective on Chinook and steelhead in the Central Valley of California: San Francisco Estuary and Watershed Science, v. 4, no. 3, p. 1–398.

Appendix A

Table A1. Parameter estimates (SE) under the reduced model for releases of acoustically tagged late-fall juvenile Chinook salmon in December, 2009 (R_1 and R_2) and February, 2010 (R_3 and R_4).

[Parameters not estimated are indicated by an "NA" in the estimate column, and parameters fixed at a constant value are noted by an "NA" in parentheses]

Parameter	R_1	R_2	R_3	R_4
S_{A1}	0.683 (0.036)	0.806 (0.032)	1.050 (0.061)	0.951 (0.018)
S_{A2}	0.981 (0.013)	0.878 (0.031)	1.052 (0.100)	0.944 (0.039)
S_{A3}	0.944 (0.025)	0.990 (0.013)	0.813 (0.104)	1.011 (0.098)
$S_{A4, open}$	0.932 (0.099)	NA	NA	NA
$S_{A4, closed}$	0.915 (0.053)	0.816 (0.067)	0.838 (0.069)	0.790 (0.097)
S_{A7}	0.893 (0.053)	0.910 (0.059)	0.856 (0.034)	0.899 (0.034)
S_{A8}	0.784 (0.061)	0.817 (0.064)	0.860 (0.035)	0.876 (0.034)
S_{B11}	0.733 (0.114)	0.696 (0.091)	0.748 (0.128)	0.876 (0.089)
S_{B12}	0.900 (0.095)	0.800 (0.126)	0.933 (0.064)	0.900 (0.067)
S_{B13}	0.690 (0.163)	0.654 (0.180)	0.797 (0.101)	0.881 (0.083)
S_{B21}	1.000 (NA)	0.899 (0.107)	0.840 (0.122)	1.000 (NA)
S_{B22}	1.000 (NA)	0.852 (0.097)	0.903 (0.057)	0.867 (0.073)
S_{B23}	0.941 (0.091)	1.000 (NA)	0.944 (0.035)	0.982 (0.054)
S_{C1}	0.750 (0.217)	NA	NA	NA
$S_{D1,Sac,open}$	1.000 (NA)	NA	NA	NA
$S_{D1,Sac,closed}$	0.870 (0.070)	0.889 (0.057)	0.962 (0.197)	0.804 (0.082)
$S_{D1,Geo}$	0.667 (0.058)	0.757 (0.052)	NA	NA
$S_{D2,Sac}$	0.883 (0.052)	0.837 (0.051)	0.714 (0.171)	1.017 (0.102)
$S_{D2,Geo}$	0.883 (0.052)	0.837 (0.051)	NA	NA
$S_{D4,Sac}$	0.360 (0.062)	0.511 (0.065)	0.313 (0.116)	0.448 (0.100)
$S_{D4,Geo}$	0.360 (0.062)	0.511 (0.065)	NA	NA
$S_{D7,Sac}$	1.000 (NA)	0.800 (0.079)	1.000 (NA)	0.908 (0.107)
$S_{D7,Geo}$	1.000 (NA)	0.800 (0.079)	NA	NA
$S_{E1,D7,Sac}$	0.640 (0.202)	0.799 (0.210)	0.482 (0.109)	0.701 (0.173)
$S_{E1,D7,Geo}$	0.640 (0.202)	0.799 (0.210)	NA	NA
$S_{E1,A8,Sac}$	1.000 (NA)	0.523 (0.153)	1.000 (NA)	1.000 (NA)
$S_{E1,A8,Geo}$	1.000 (NA)	0.523 (0.153)	NA	NA
ω_{open}	0.185 (0.043)	0.000 (NA)	0.000 (NA)	0.000 (NA)
Ψ_{A1}	0.777 (0.039)	0.681 (0.043)	0.553 (0.049)	0.779 (0.030)
Ψ_{B11}	0.134 (0.032)	0.243 (0.044)	0.242 (0.091)	0.135 (0.027)
Ψ_{B21}	0.089 (0.027)	0.076 (0.028)	0.205 (0.085)	0.086 (0.022)
$\Psi_{A2,open}$	0.671 (0.121)	NA	NA	NA
$\Psi_{A2,closed}$	0.656 (0.058)	0.575 (0.055)	0.812 (0.037)	0.770 (0.038)
$\Psi_{C2,open}$	0.263 (0.113)	NA	NA	NA
$\Psi_{D2,open}$	0.066 (0.064)	NA	NA	NA
$\Psi_{D2,closed}$	0.344 (0.058)	0.425 (0.055)	0.188 (0.037)	0.230 (0.038)
$\phi_{B21,B12}$	0.100 (0.095)	0.000 (NA)	0.000 (NA)	0.000 (NA)
$\phi_{B21,B22}$	0.900 (0.095)	0.899 (0.107)	0.840 (0.122)	1.000 (NA)
$\phi_{B11,B12}$	0.600 (0.126)	0.346 (0.093)	0.290 (0.123)	0.741 (0.116)
$\phi_{B11,B22}$	0.133 (0.088)	0.350 (0.095)	0.458 (0.143)	0.135 (0.089)
$\phi_{A7,A8}$	0.796 (0.060)	0.769 (0.067)	0.700 (0.038)	0.811 (0.039)
$\phi_{A7,E1}$	0.096 (0.038)	0.141 (0.054)	0.156 (0.033)	0.088 (0.029)
$\phi_{D4,D7,Sac}$	0.266 (0.056)	0.339 (0.059)	0.250 (0.109)	0.325 (0.093)

$\phi_{D4,D7,Geo}$	0.266 (0.056)	0.339 (0.059)	NA	NA
$\phi_{D4,E1,Sac}$	0.094 (0.037)	0.172 (0.048)	0.063 (0.061)	0.124 (0.059)
$\phi_{D4,E1,Geo}$	0.094 (0.037)	0.172 (0.048)	NA	NA
P_{A2}	0.946 (0.021)	0.915 (0.026)	0.180 (0.026)	0.823 (0.027)
P_{A3}	1.000 (NA)	1.000 (NA)	0.171 (0.036)	0.340 (0.039)
P_{A4}	0.979 (0.021)	0.985 (0.015)	0.329 (0.053)	0.156 (0.036)
P_{A7}	0.754 (0.057)	0.651 (0.066)	0.855 (0.030)	0.702 (0.041)
$P_{A8,Sac}$	0.845 (0.054)	0.858 (0.057)	0.953 (0.022)	0.927 (0.029)
$P_{A8,Geo}$	1.000 (NA)	0.858 (0.057)	NA	NA
$P_{A9,Sac}$	0.860 (0.049)	0.894 (0.041)	0.901 (0.030)	0.906 (0.030)
$P_{A9,Geo}$	1.000 (NA)	0.894 (0.041)	NA	NA
P_{B11}	1.000 (NA)	0.900 (0.095)	0.211 (0.094)	0.500 (0.107)
P_{B12}	1.000 (NA)	1.000 (NA)	0.778 (0.098)	0.900 (0.067)
P_{B21}	1.000 (NA)	1.000 (0.186)	0.248 (0.113)	0.627 (0.133)
P_{B22}	1.000 (NA)	0.933 (0.064)	0.372 (0.059)	0.906 (0.063)
P_{B13}	1.000 (NA)	1.000 (NA)	1.000 (NA)	1.000 (NA)
P_{B23}	0.727 (0.134)	0.258 (0.112)	0.910 (0.049)	0.945 (0.053)
P_{C1}	1.000 (NA)	1.000 (NA)	1.000 (NA)	1.000 (NA)
P_{D1}	1.000 (NA)	0.985 (0.015)	0.944 (0.054)	0.867 (0.062)
$P_{D2,Sac}$	1.000 (NA)	0.956 (0.025)	0.312 (0.116)	0.431 (0.090)
$P_{D2,Geo}$	0.895 (0.050)	0.956 (0.025)	NA	NA
$P_{D4,Geo}$	0.837 (0.073)	0.917 (0.046)	NA	NA
$P_{D4,Sac}$	1.000 (NA)	0.917 (0.046)	1.000 (NA)	0.848 (0.098)
$P_{D7,Geo}$	0.853 (0.078)	1.000 (NA)	NA	NA
$P_{D7,Sac}$	0.853 (0.078)	0.816 (0.104)	0.793 (0.106)	0.460 (0.126)
$P_{E1,Sac}$	0.866 (0.124)	0.521 (0.160)	0.823 (0.112)	0.697 (0.118)
$P_{E1,Geo}$	1.000 (NA)	1.000 (NA)	NA	NA
λ_{Sac}	0.902 (0.038)	0.834 (0.048)	0.849 (0.035)	0.777 (0.039)
λ_{Geo}	0.902 (0.038)	0.834 (0.048)	NA	NA